IoT DISRUPTIONS 2020

Connected World of 2020 with
Deep Learning IoT

Stanford Edition

BY SUDHA JAMTHE

IoT Disruptions 2020

Published by Sudha Jamthe

Editor: Hiru Létap

Foreword: Marsha Collier

Epilogue: Rob Van Kranenburg

Cover Design: Neha Jamthe

Image Credit: "agsandrew/shutterstock"

ISBN: 978-1519503411

Book Website: **http://www.iotdisruptions.com**

The author and publisher do not assume and hereby disclaim any liability to any party for any loss, damage, or disruption caused by errors or omissions, whether such errors or omissions result from negligence, accident, or any other cause.

First Published: March 2016

DEDICATION

To my Stanford Students, The IoT Business Makers of 2020

CONTENTS

Foreword by Marsha Collier

The Internet of Thing is everywhere. To the well informed, it just may be the next big thing, but it's not yet as readily identifiable to the public sector. Adoption and understanding will take time. The everyday consumer looks at innovations like Wi-Fi enabled thermostats, cameras and maybe lights that connect to their home router without an understanding of the big picture. The exact definition of "IoT" is not yet widely known.

Realize that we are on the cutting edge; just scratching the surface of this new technology and way of life. Innovators must build the products and get them adopted. Product managers and students are charged with finding new and creative ways to adapt the data to create the future.

In this book, Sudha Jamthe analyzes the future of where this challenge can take us. She examines the existing landscape of opportunities for data and technology professionals and hones in on the best direction for our endeavors.

I have known Sudha for many years and she is highly respected for her insights in developing products for the 21st century. She really is a visionary, able to spot new technology trends in the social and mobile arenas. Read this book slowly and digest her advice. I suspect you will refer back to it many times.

- Marsha Collier, Best Selling Author (47 books), Computer and Technology Radio Host and Futurist

CHAPTER 1 Breaking the Human-Machine Fabric – Welcome to 2020

Welcome to the new world of connected devices. Internet of Things (IoT) is making every 'thing' on us, inside us and all around us, smart by adding sensors and Internet connectivity. Our home, cars, pacemakers and even our shoes are becoming smart with Internet of Things (IoT). Smart things are beginning to interact with us using voice, facial recognition and gesture control. Machine learning and Deep learning are the latest technologies that teach computers to develop smart algorithms to make smart devices intelligent to give us sound advice. When connected IoT devices all around us become intelligent it will change the human-machine interface. If human intelligence can be replicated, and human experience can be deep learned, the barrier between man and machine will begin to crumble.

IoT devices are sensing our environments with gesture computing, feeling our emotions with affective computing and personalizing our experiences with recognition computing. Will this stop at human-machine interactions, or are we helping machines develop self-awareness with personality and opinions, to become our friends, partners and part of our families. There is no escape from the trajectory of change of our perceptions of our worlds and us as humans. Or is there?

The fact that you are reading this book tells me that you love new technology. You do not stop at buying the latest wearable devices and playing with new gadgets. You want more. You yearn to find out new opportunities and business models ahead of everyone else.

Internet of Things is bringing new waves of innovation in the form of startups, funding from Venture Capitalists, innovative changes in existing Internet architecture with new standards, new layers of software, new hardware, new distribution channels and new evolving business models. I absolutely do not believe that this is going to eliminate jobs by giving it to Robots. It has actually begun opening up so many new opportunities to innovate, creating new jobs.

One more thing I know about you. You are creative and do not stop at learning about new technologies. You are an architect and want to be a driver of change to build out the opportunity in this technology.

In the following chapters I will show you what areas of the promise of the IoT is scaling up to solve real customer problems. Let me tell you upfront. Robots are not going to reduce jobs available for humans. I have a chapter on the new landscape of jobs. Big Data and analytics is the backbone of IoT devices so analysts and machine learning jobs are scaling. Students are lucky to skip old technologies and are at an advantage to ride the new wave of Internet of Things Innovation. So I have added a section to outline IoT jobs for Students.

As you flip the pages of this book, **join me to step into a magical world of inspiration as we look into what will be the world landscape in 2020.** The connected world of 2020 will offer new ways of living with Smart super markets, Digital Health, change and growth in Industries – Auto, Oil and Gas, Consumer Home, Connected Car, Connected Cities, Textile, Shipping, Logistics and Manufacturing. **I have a chapter on the issues of privacy and insurance disruptions** with Auto, Healthcare, Property and Life for the connected world customer. **Finally join me to carve a path to 2020 with Machine Learning, Deep Learning, and Algorithms.**

Audience for this book:

This book is for –

- My Stanford students from the IoT Business class who have been my inspiration, ever curious to understand the IoT ecosystem to stake their place in it with their promising business plans.
- Entrepreneurs, Strategists and Technologists from hardware and software background looking for a vision of the connected world of 2020 to fill in the gaps with innovative products and services.
- Students trying to figure out where are the jobs in IoT and what skills will be needed as the IoT adoption scales mainstream.
- Data Analysts who are learning machine learning and want to understand their business applications in IoT.
- Product Managers, Business Managers, Technology Strategists, Analysts, BPM specialists in Consumer and Enterprise space looking for ideas and inspiration on how IoT will transform their industries for Retail/Supermarkets, Healthcare, Manufacturing, Oil and Gas, Textile, Logistics, Farms, and Consumer Home, Car and City.
- This is not meant as a book for programmers looking for sample code and tools to build out machine learning for the IoT ecosystem.

CHAPTER 2 The Promise of The Internet of Things

2.1 What is IoT?

Internet of Things or IoT for short covers a wide a range of devices that have added sensors and communication to the Internet, and solve problems that were not possible before.

My car broke down and I rushed to take it for service before the dealer closed for the weekend. I left home and forgot to close my garage and rushed back to double check and close it. While I waited for my car I remembered we had run out of pet food, soap and coffee and did a run to the market to buy them. I came home and found that I had locked myself out and had left my keys inside. I went to pickup my spouse from airport hoping to use his keys but his flight was delayed because of an emergency maintenance in his aircraft. We have to keep track of so many things because all things all around us are un-smart.

I wish I lived in a world where my car would take care of its own service; my garage would close automatically when I leave home, and my household appliances would order refills. Planes would never be late and factories would not slow down for maintenance. My doctor would check my health remotely without me ever thinking about it.

This is not a futuristic world.

It gets even better. My home would know when I enter and unlock doors for me and lights would turn on automatically. It will even know if I returned after a workout and turn my thermostat to a comfortable setting. My pet feeder would have fed my cat and she will nuzzle around my feet. In the morning my alarm will tell the coffeemaker and toaster when I am getting up so my breakfast will be ready for me.

This does not stop at my home. My car would offer intelligent guidance during long drives and park for me in a hurry. My clothes will track my biometrics and inform my doctor that I am healthy. If

I ever need physiotherapy, my Wii will inform my doctor of my progress. No mechanical part would fail in a factory, aircraft, dam, a shipment container or an oil rig because they will all be intelligent to predict part failures and replace themselves proactively.

Won't such an intelligent world run so smoothly and free up time for us for so much more creativity?

Internet of Things (IoT) has begun creating this convenient world for us by making ordinary things we carry on us and around us smart by adding sensors to track and fix problems before they arise. This opens us to a whole new world of conveniences not earlier possible when our toothbrush and toasters just did their boring old mechanical actions.

I would call IoT transformative because it is changing our world to run so smoothly and disrupting many industries. Now we have technology that will help devices communicate with us and with each other and helps them develop algorithms that makes them intelligence to predict problems before they arise and solve them.

Join me to learn about how IoT is disrupting our future society, economies and the very fabric of man-machine interface.

2.2 Market Size and Value Creation

'There will between 26 to 50 Billion IoT devices in the world by 2020 [1] which translates to 6 devices per person on the planet.

By 2018 companies that started 3 years earlier will provide 50% of IoT solutions. [2]

This means that companies starting now are going to offer 50% of all IoT solutions in 2 years from now, on their way to serving a world of 50 Billion IoT devices in 2020. IoT growth is led by product innovations and cost efficiencies.

Value is created with IoT devices at the sensors, at the communication layer by sharing information to users to take near real-time action and by analytics insights from huge volume of data. For example Amazon Dash is IoT Device that signals the depletion of pet supply and re-orders them creates value.

In Boeing, where sensors signal faulty equipment and communicate it in real-time to get the aircraft fixed quickly, the value is created in the communication. In Healthcare, the analysis of a patient's health data integrated with their health history saves lives creating value in the data from analytics insights.

This value creation is expediting us to the connected world of 2020 to new ways of living, changing our social fabric and changing human relationship with machines.

2.3 Technologies Underlying Intelligent IoT

Imagine your garage opener. Prior to IoT, we pushed a remote button and voilà it opened your garage. This was proprietary communication between the mechanical remote and the garage door using RF communication with a Radio transmitter, similar to how our telephone handset communicates to its base.

By making the garage a smart IoT device, the same push of the garage button happens from a mobile App that communicates to the garage via the Internet using Wi-Fi or Bluetooth and magically transforms a software electric signal to a mechanical switch to open or close the garage. In laymen language the IoT smart garage monitors itself whether it was left open beyond a certain pre-set threshold time and notifies the user who can remotely close it and continue on her jolly way. In technology terms it is a miracle to get an electric pulse from a software app to create a mechanical movement in a faraway garage hub to make it close the garage. I am not even getting into how the garage monitored itself for being left open and sent a notification to a software app far away. This same technology applies to monitoring dams and bridges before they break or to improve efficiencies in factories by tracking manufacturing lines for quality, compliance and prevent machine failures before they happen.

Join me in marveling at the layers of technologies. It includes embedded devices, communication with Bluetooth or Wi-Fi, security software, data analytics, cloud infrastructure, notifications, integration of hardware and software, cool consumer design, intelligent programmatic actions, mobile software app, chip and system processing power converting between electric microprocessor signals to mechanical switch or relay movement to make our device do what it did manually, Machine to Machine (M2M) communications, voice recognition machine learning and artificial intelligence.

2.4 Applications Taking Us to the World of 2020

The breadth of Applications from IoT is another reason to learn about its impact on innovations and how it will impact our lives by 2020. It covers Wearables on us and inside us and Quantified Self, Connected home, Connected cars and Self Driving Cars, Smart cities, the Industrial IoT and Intelligent Drones, Robots and Algorithms.

Wearables are IoT Products worn by babies, adults, seniors and pets. These typically include fitbands, watches, health sensors, and devices embedded in clothing and accessories that we wear on ourselves. Wearable applications are exploding as they tap into consumer pains and passions left unsolved by the Internet by creating value from the data from the always-on connectivity.

"Wearables and the IoT are rapidly altering the landscape of everyday life, fashioning innovative paths to wellness, productivity, and creativity. Wearables and the IoT are affecting more than step counts and heart rates — every industry is being changed through the use of the information gathered from IoT devices and sensors." says Scott Amyx, CEO Amyx McKinsey and Wearable and IoT Thought Leader.

Quantified self refers to the movement where we collect and analyze data about our bodies. Quantified self makes us willingly put our life under scrutiny by IoT devices watching did we sleep well, brush our teeth the right way, eat the right kind of foods, are we hydrated, what are our health vitals, are we in danger and do we need to call for help and whether we are sleeping, breathing and exercising for optimal living.

Wearables inside us are ingested or implanted inside us. They add a new set of biometrics that was not collected so frequently. We have IoT devices that track our cortisol level in our brains, bacteria in our gut and insulin levels in our blood giving us the ability to quantify our vitals and to help us manage our lives with awareness and live longer.

There are wearables that are called nanobots that roam the insides of our bodies detecting and killing cancer cells. There are medical devices such as pace makers that we implant inside our bodies that are now connected to the Internet and share information about our health to our care providers helping accelerate research and prolong lives.

Connected Home or Smart Buildings makes our appliances smart and creates new conveniences and solves for frustrations that we have learned to live with.

These include our thermostat that knows when we are away and sets the right temperature, security cameras monitoring our homes outside and inside, smart toaster, smart fridge, smart coffeemaker, pet dispenser and dishwashers that can order refills taking the guess out of our daily lives.

It also covers our smart garages and smart locks and power saving smart lights and garden watering systems solving for problems that we didn't even dream was solvable.

Companies such as Philips, Sharp and Belkin have jumped into the foray modifying their proprietary remote and hub systems to become Internet savvy but still keeping it proprietary communication between their remote and hubs. Whole foray of startups are innovating with room for lot more to solve for problems local and global in nature.

There is a whole open source movement and open hub solutions evolving to make the Internet hub controlling multiple devices open communication standards thereby slashing the cost of Connected Home Hubs.

As our homes and office buildings become connected smart buildings, it goes beyond individual devices but the office, factory or home becomes a 'Thing" with intelligence that has many devices that talks to each other and makes decisions for us based on our habits. Our interaction with our smart home will be so different from our current interactions and whole new business models and services have to evolve to build upon this connectivity into our homes and lives.

Smart office buildings and factories will monitor and maintain themselves for energy savings, ergonomics and improved safety. Smart chairs, smart sprinkler systems, and smart manufacturing lines and wearables for factories will communicate with each other to create efficiencies and better working environments.

Connected Cars and Self-Driving Cars

Cars have begun becoming smart with Internet connectivity and in most cases it is not even marketed to the average car buyer. Tesla has been the unrivaled leader of the connected car space. In Nov 2015 Tesla introduced their Autopilot mode for the S Series making it a self-driving car in a limited sense with a simple over-the-air software update to the cars.

Connected cars send vehicle diagnostics to the dealer for fleet maintenance proactively and offer entertainment, weather, and traffic information on our cars. AT&T offers an automotive development platform that is used by Tesla Motors. The operating system in the Tesla car is remotely updated similar to an Apple Phone OS update without the need to visit the dealer.

European Union has a mandatory requirement for all calls to be equipped with eCall, an emergency smart car service that calls the nearest emergency center and sends minimum data including car location in the case of a collision. This has speeded up smart cars deployments in Europe. There are emergency drones being tested to help save lives during road accidents with remote health diagnostics.

Some car manufacturers are opting to provide basic apps with the cars while others plan to update Apps using wireless networks to keep the apps up to date in cars. The connected car needs a wireless service to communicate with the Internet. This is posing a challenge because consumers are used to paying one-time purchase price for a car while connected car services will require monthly payments like a Phone service. Nissan's Leaf EV cars come with AT&T 2G network paid for by Nissan. When AT&T expires the 2G network in 2017, the car's connection will stop working unless upgraded to a 3G network. The verdict is out on who will bear the cost of the connectivity of connected cars and how this will play out as a business model in car sales.

Self-driving cars are autonomous Robots that can learn driving in a consumer setting. Did you know that self-driving cars just do not learn road rules? Instead they have been introduced scenarios such a golf cart crossing their path to allow them to learn what they need to learn to understand human traffic patterns using Machine Learning Algorithms.

Bicycles, boats, and ships are also becoming smart and connected. Drones are being launched as unmanned transportation devices in rough terrains. They are all more then hardware and software. They are machine learning to become intelligent to master their environments.

As you read on, join me to think of this not as a connected car space but as modern transportation in a connected world.

As the car, bike and trucks become connected and self-driving, the entire city infrastructure and our habits have to change to new ways of lives.

Smart City

A smart city has sensors for traffic monitoring, smart lighting, smart meter of city parking slots, and informs residents about air quality, noise levels and pedestrian traffic levels. Barcelona has become a connected city with smart waste management and smart parking meters and smart bus stops operating on citywide Wi-Fi. Izmir city in Turkey is deploying smart traffic lights and smart real-time traffic guidance for emergency vehicles. Transpose India a connected city project from CEPT University, Ahmadabad, India has developed intelligent sensors to monitor data to understand traffic patterns and consumer driving patterns to solve for traffic congestion. Smart IoT devices provide constant data to help residents find parking spots, and get information about commuter options. It helps the city officials with urban planning and crime prevention by looking at data trends to spot pockets in the city that need their attention.

Urban Informatics refers to the data a city collects to create transparency and solve problems for its citizens. This includes data from sensors for traffic monitoring, smart lighting, city parking usage patterns, air quality data, noise levels and pedestrian traffic levels. The challenges of building a connected or smart city lie in change management in a city among multiple stakeholders, lack of clarity of who owns the new infrastructure costs and need to bring citizens to participate and utilize the new smart products to generate scale of adoption while maintaining the very fabric that makes the city.

The challenges do not lie in the technical ability of the city to measure city data but it measuring it correctly and in presenting the data using a common language among stakeholders who are not used to work together.

City of Amsterdam has created the World's First Internet of Things lab called iBeacon Living Lab (http://ibeaconlivinglab.com/) and the Beacon Mile. This is a set of sensors along a public path including a library, a canal, a bicycle bridge and museum. They have made it open source for the public to access these beacons to test out use cases for a connected city that goes beyond large business to social good apps. This has further inspired entrepreneurs to create The Things Network (a public network of LoRA WAN gateways to create a crowd sourced open source IoT connectivity for the whole city of Amsterdam. This is a classic example of an IoT Disruption that started with a city and a citizen now creating a new innovation movement globally.

Industrial IoT

Factories are using IoT devices to track thresholds for predictive maintenance and build in factory automations and bring supply chain efficiencies.

Solar panels on our rooftops, electric vehicle charger such as Blink or Charge Point are all smart devices sending information on our consumption patterns for service efficiency. Pacific Gas and Electric PG&E has switched to smart meters that send them hourly meter readings. Now we can see our energy usage patterns. The electric company gets automatic outage detection. They can now offer better service and charge us with a metered rating per hour tailored to our usage.

GE has instrumented sensors in equipments and collects and analyses massive volume of data to predict and improve performance. TempuTech is a grain management and hazard monitoring company for agricultural storage customers. It uses GE's Intelligent Platforms and uses IoT sensors to check for humidity, broken grain elevators and sends alerts and gets fixes to create operational efficiencies and hazard prevention.

Industrial IoT has many evolving business models. Karsten Königstein CEO of Smartly Solutions from Germany who worked with Bosch says, "IoT can offer many value with measurable ROI. It offers two way digital communications inside the factory floor replacing paper. It helps logistics track stock in the production floor and also during transportation. More business models will evolve in industries as we test and iterate new innovation with Internet of Things."

Voice and Communication are important technologies needed to provide communication between device and humans and between devices. Ken Herron of Unified Inbox calls this the 'Social IoT' where we need communication platforms to allow devices to communicate with us at the right time, in the right medium (chat, email, notifications), with the right level of urgency for different device communication scenarios. This could also be machine learned to optimize for different customer preferences for different device usage scenarios.

Artificial Intelligence and Augmented Reality are two technologies that are in research mode innovating and finding applications in home and factories. Factories have introduced smart devices in their production lines. These alert employees about machine downtimes before they happen and improve efficiencies. Oil and Gas, Mining industries are employing sensors to track for critical machine's health and predict and avoid downtimes. Farms are becoming smart with connected granary and smart watering systems.

Konica Minolta offers Augmented reality in Oil and Gas industry to expedite fixing of broken critical machinery. Christian Mastrodonato Chief Technologist of Konica Minolta says "With IoT and sensors you can predict parts failure. With Augmented Reality, you can have real intervention, have real intervention by real people who know how the system works and fix the right parts quickly and efficiently".

Shipping and Logistics business uses several sensors in containers and tracks the data to improve efficiencies. Textile industry uses RFID to track containers and is adding sensors to finished clothing to create wearables tracking health vitals.

Qualcomm has built mobile and hospital health management platforms to connect patients and care providers in securely ways offering remote continuous care for critical patients taking IoT devices home. Hospitals also do predictive analytics with healthcare data to find high-risk patients and provide them care proactively.

[1.] Gartner Press Release 2013 estimated 26 Bil devices & Cisco estimates 50Bil devices by 2020 & [2] Gartner at Tech Europe

CHAPTER 3 Digital Health

"Smart mobile health platforms can act as integrators connecting data gathered from IoT devices and health data such as blood tests, medical history and genetics, environmental, social economics data. They can then analyze these data and its impact on causation, treatment and outcome of diseases and provide personalized recommendations to patients" - Tatyana Kanzaveli Founder and CEO, Open Health Network.

Health was the first industry where Internet of Things touched consumers directly and is the top industry disrupted because it has woken up consumers about the power of their health data.

Internet of Things came to Healthcare in the form of wearable Fitness Trackers. Now we are seeing non-fitness personal products and a new type of wearables that are inside our bodies. This has created the new area of Digital Health.

3.1 Wearables and Health Informatics

Wearables like Fitbit started tracking the fitness health of users with social features to share their data to friends. It has expanded to track health vitals such as pulse, blood pressure etc. beyond exercising to daily health monitoring. Health tracking started with the early adopters of exercise conscious adults and has expanded to health monitoring for seniors, babies and pets. Today it includes sleep monitoring and provides data about sleep cycles leading to questions about stress and lifestyle of the individual impacting their health.

Apple offers the Apple Watch as a wearable device, Healthkit for developers and Health App for users of iOS devices.

Apple Watch measures all the ways a user moves. It differentiates between walking the dog, climbing stairs, or playing with kids. Health kit allows iOS apps from developers that collect health and fitness information to store user data securely in a central location and gives control to users on what app can share what data with Apple's Health App. For example I use Steps+ App to track how I meet my 10,000 steps goals each day and SleepTime App to monitor my sleeping pattern and see a combined dashboard in the Health App on my iPhone.

All wearables are not fitness bands. Imec offers an EKG necklace and Preventive checks for cardiac monitoring, arrhythmia detection, stress monitoring, and epilepsy monitoring. Neumitra's biowatch measures the sympathetic nervous system to track stress. Traditional Health devices such as Omar Blood Pressure monitor have added Bluetooth Connectivity to track history of the BP data collected. The vast volume of data is enriching the field of health informatics.

Power of Health Informatics

The real power of Health tracking wearables and other connected health devices lies in the data they provide. Storage and processing of health data is called Health Informatics.

Health Informatics is empowering consumers in three ways today.

(i) Consumers using various wearable fitness trackers are becoming more health conscious as they are seeing their own fitness data daily and are comparing them with friends in social networks. Access to our own health data is empowering us to have a dialog with our doctors to make informed healthcare choices. Recently, I saw my pulse shoot up when I checked my blood pressure at home. When I visited the doctor my pulse levels were normal. I started wearing a Basis Peak wearable watch and could track the trend of my pulse and went back to my doctor to have an informed discussion and ask questions about my health care options.

(ii) Hospitals can track the health of patients while they are in the comfort of their homes by providing them with wearables that send them data about their biometrics and vitals. Access to continuous health data is allowing for continuous care of critical patients by hospitals. This is saving cost of unnecessary hospitalization and saving lives when urgent intervention is needed.

(iii) The volume of health data from connected health devices is contributing to speed up health research.

Telehealth and Telemedicine

Telehealth is an evolving branch of Digital Health which educates and encourages users to connect wearables to provide data to connect to healthcare systems or offers remote diagnosis by physicians. Pediatricians can now look into the ears of kids for ear-infection remotely using smart otoscopes.

3.2 Wearables Inside Us

A new class of Digital Health products are evolving as wearables not on us but inside us.

3.2.1 Cyber implants

Boston University is testing a bionic pancreas with an implantable needle that talks to a Phone and tracks blood sugar levels. Proteus Health offers a FDA approved pill with Ingestion Event Markers to track user's biometrics from inside their bodies. Digital tattoos from Motorola and Vivalink has a NFC based skin tag to unlock your phone securely.

University of Illinois has created a skin implant that is a mesh of computer fibers thinner than a human hair that can monitor our body's inner workings from the surface. The Gates Foundation is supporting a MIT project to create an implantable female contraceptive.

3.2.2 Implanted Digital Identity or Verified Self

Swarms of nano-devices called "motes" can organize themselves inside the human body to attack cancer cells or store our information inside us encrypted to store our secure identity. Implanting RFID chips to track a person has uses in tracking military soldiers or a lost child but has serious implications for the privacy of the individual and societal impact of avoiding an Orwelian society.

3.3 Wearables that extend the Brain to IoT

A Brown University project now owned by Braingate, has created a brain implant called Braingate. When this sensor is implanted into the brain it monitors brain activity and converts the thoughts or neural signals into computer commands.

The sensor consists of 100 thin electrodes and an external prosthetic decoder device. This is in clinical trials to help patients with ALS or Spinal cord injury. Think of the products you can build with this to help disabled people to operate wheelchairs or move other things around them by their thoughts.

3.4 Digital Informatics Insights and Deep Learning

There is so much data from wearables, from smart weighing scales, smart toothbrushes, wireless glucose monitors etc. This contributes to the rich field of bio Informatics.

There are three open opportunities being built out in healthcare space.

First all fitness devices provide raw data trends and stop short of providing actionable insights. What will help the user is to understand the insights behind the data to offer actionable insights. For example Sleep monitors show how many times a user was awake during the night. So its interesting data to know you were stressed and tossing and turning at night. If the health device can provide insight behind the data and tell the user when to get help from their physician, and provide details on their sleep patterns and the impact stress will have on their overall health it will drive actions that was not possible with the IoT.

Secondly the data collected from IoT is about the user's action or what can be gathered live from sensors. Today This data is presented in isolation from the user's healthcare data that tells about their health vitals, health history and any conditions they are getting treatment from their medical practitioners. **Integration of these two data will provide useful insights that can help the user much more holistically and drive actions that were not possible without the IoT device**. This integration has to be done at the cloud by health platforms or health cloud providers. It comes with huge opportunities but also huge challenges of managing the privacy of the user and compliance about protecting their right to who can access their health information.

With wearable market highly fragmented there are many different wearable fitness bands that send data to many different cloud storage platforms. This adds to the complexity of integrating the wearables data to legacy healthcare systems.

Thirdly, Machine Learning applied to health data helps with predicting onset of diseases, looking for pathogens in blood samples and finding cancer cells inside a person. This area is ripe for innovation with deep learning.

3.5 Shifts in jobs in Healthcare

Healthcare traditionally is a conservative field in technology adoption because the limitation of privacy and compliance rules related to patient data. Healthcare platforms are evolving to provide web integrations to healthcare systems. These jobs will shift to people who can understand client based IoT devices data and consumer sensibilities related to knowing proactive information about their health.

A health conscious customer is a more demanding customer who will want to take charge of their healthcare management with need for more education and expect more open conversation with health practitioners.

This will **impact the role of healthcare professionals not only technologists to become more tech savvy about the role and data from IoT devices.**

There is much opportunity for **big data analysts** to provide insights from the health data from fitness tracker devices. There is an untapped potential for **developers** to build new apps using Apple WatchKit to solve solutions in healthcare using the health tracking space.

System integrators and health platform provides who understand the privacy and compliance issues with healthcare who can now understand IoT and integrate both data from IoT devices and the patient's healthcare data in a meaningful way have so many startup and job opportunities **to build cloud infrastructure, data integration**, data analytics to develop and present insights.

Machine Learning of Healthcare data is beginning to make predictive analytics of cancer in at-risk patients to get them proactive treatment thereby saving lives.

CHAPTER 4 Smart Super Markets

"Today's students are digital natives. We have integrated mobile technology into our lives. With the inception of the Internet of Things, digital native graduates are at the intersection of a new industry that will make us question why everything is not connected to our devices." - Paul Heayn, mobile product manager

It is a retailers dream to know their customer behavior as they navigate through the purchase funnel from traffic to consideration to purchase. IoT devices collect massive volume of data about customers. The key in understanding opportunities in Retail and IoT is connectivity. IoT offer three types of connectivity, each with its own set of opportunities.

4.1 Pervasive Connectivity

Internet of Things offers multiple customer touch points while the customer deliberates a purchase. IoT devices provide data while the customer jogs, sleeps, eats and walks. **A connected customer is an engaged customer because each touch point gives data insights about the customer's behavior.** This will help the retailer understand the customer better and reduce friction in the commerce experience and personalize the customer's optimal experience flow to purchase and retention.

IoT has taken the Commerce experience from 1-click to 0-click commerce. The Amazon Dash Button is a classic example of that. It allows customers to tap a button pre-programmed to order commodity items around the house. Your coffee maker orders coffee, washer orders soap, fridge orders eggs, medicine cabinets order medicine prescription and pet dispenser re-orders pet food.

This is what I call as 0-click commerce, total frictionless commerce. This is action by the customer pre-decided to trust Amazon to order refills once the item reaches a certain inventory level made possible only by the proliferation of smart devices connected to the Internet.

4.2 Contextual Connectivity

IoT provides data along with context of the customer. **It tells us the location of the customer, their moods and how focused the customer** is. For example a Fitbit does not only show the numbers of steps taken and calories burnt but consistency of such behavior indicates that the customer is a much more deliberate focused person. A customer who is able to focus their health habits to consistency is likely to show a focused behavior on their research to purchase a product than do binge shopping or buy random things. This impacts the experience that should be provided in the purchase flow for the customer instead of dependency on merchandising for cross-sells.

4.3. Data from Multiple Connected Devices

Join me in imagining the story from the data from wearable devices differently. The fitness tracker will tell you more about your moods than just track how much you walked today. Health and sleep monitor tells you more about behavior and intent than just health. Is the customer running for health or is she running to get relief from stress? Retailers strive to learn their customer's behaviors intimately because it drives shopping revenues. Is the health conscious customer doing targeted shopping, a deliberate list based shopping with focus or is the customer doing binge shopping is driven by emotions?

4.4 Future of Retail with Smart Super Markets

Innovation is ripe in retail untapped by Internet of Thing devices. Here are some of the opportunities I can see. Sky is the limit to what else is possible once retailers develop a better understanding of their customers and customers get used to being always on and communicating their behavior shifts to retailers demanding more from store, mobile, online retail Omni-channel customer experiences.

Retailers can know when a customer is in their store by using Geofencing on IoT devices. Estimote offers one such device that restaurants can place in tables and allows customer to pay from their seats using a mobile app. Coupa Café in Palo Alto, California is an example of a restaurant who uses Estimote for geofencing making the food ordering and payment frictionless in ways not possible without smart connected devices.

In recent times, Target, Home Depot and Macys, all large retailer chains in America and Altromercato the Italian retailer with 300 chain stores have setup Bluetooth sensors called "Beacons" in select stores to connect to customer apps to create customized experiences based on geofencing customers. Altromercato uses facial recognition to understand customer demographics to adapt their inventory and shelf displays. They have the ability to collect data about customer behavior in their stores to learn about customer's shopping habits inside their stores.

Pizzahut in China has setup beacons from Sensoria in hundreds of stores and created a geo-fencing experience in WeChat, the popular messaging app. It uses this to offer coupons and sharing opportunity for users thereby measuring consumer preference of food in real-time.

A startup called Sense360 offers behavioral data about customers from a combination of sensors inside their iPhones to create invisible apps that connect to other mobile apps at gas stations, stores and libraries.

KLM Airlines deployed beacons to provide airport navigation for passengers in transit to another terminal by using its own app. JKF airport in New York deployed a system called The BlipTrack system using beacons at TSA checkpoints that uses passenger's mobile phones to measure how long people are taking to go through the lines. Both have different technology implementations and challenges of deployment to scale. It is important to use these sensors with the permission of users; else it will break customer trust and disrupt businesses negatively.

In Jan 2016, a group of students from Friedrich Alexander University (**Universität Erlangen-Nürnberg**), Shah Asif aka Raja,

Nicole Sprengler, Danielle, Collie, Anil Maharjan from Germany dreamed up the vision of smart supermarkets of 2020. Their vision is to tag all items with RFID and make the shopping cart a smart cart. The smart cart will keep track of the customer spending by tracking what items are in the cart. It will avoid long lines or queues at checkout and eliminate checkout counters and allow paying directly from our mobile devices with smart payment options. Checkout-less checkout has been tried by retailers earlier. Today it shows more promise because of the promise of Smart IoT carts and consumer adoption of mobile payments. Blockchain offers secure M2M payment options which can also be applied to smart supermarkets.

I haven't seen my favorite use case in any store yet! Imagine if **retail store kiosks can interact with a wearable device as the user enters the store** and allows the user to order in a single click without the long process of going around the store and deliberating on purchases or to order shipping of items when the inventory is available in another store.

Chapter 5 Changing Jobs Landscape

5.1 Jobs for Humans vs. Robots

It is exaggerated when we hear about jobs going away to machines with IoT. It is true that robots and drones will create autonomous machines that can do some of the mundane jobs done by humans. Today we have robots in factories building machines or moving heavy parts.

In the future as algorithms evolve jobs with repetitive actions can be moved to machines instead of humans. Some examples are travel agents, primary care doctors, recruiting sourcers and office assistants scheduling mundane meetings. It cannot replace an office manager who brings people skills and runs an office smoothly or the experienced doctor who can do surgeries or do specialized tests or diagnosis.

Many jobs may get spread out globally with telemedicine and tele-surgery. This could help where there is shortage of doctors or specialized skills professionals. The other important impact on jobs from IoT is shifting of industries to new markets or different parts of the world. For example textile and fashion as industries are being disrupted by wearables and will shift where successful wearables are being innovated and produced in scale cost-effectively.

5.2 Changing Role of Product Managers

IoT Technologies are in early stages of evolution. The role of the Product manager that is a pivot role in technology is most important and most impacted by IoT. Product managers are needed to adapt to changes to build the product flows and optimal integration points. They are needed to adapt to the change in how IoT changes the product's interaction with customers. For example customers were used to their oven and fridges do their work quietly. Now with smart devices, the customer is empowered to get notifications alerts and data trends as part of the product experience. The role of PM will require understanding Connected smart devices and also how it should connect the commerce experience flow to desktop and mobile experiences intuitively.

"IoT solutions tend to be complex -- with local sensors, mobile apps, massively scaled cloud infrastructures and long-duration interactions. At the same time, our millions of users need simple user experiences. As today's IoT product managers, we must understand end-to-end systems and also have some design 'taste.' We have to collaborate effectively with mixed teams of developers and interaction designers. And we have to deliver products that are a joy to use – that make the wondrous look easy." – Rich Mironov long-time product management advocate and CEO, Mironov Consulting and Product Management Author

The challenge for Product Managers is also because earlier they were software or hardware product managers except for few embedded devices. **Now the Product managers have to have knowledge of embedded systems, communication layers, Internet cloud technologies and mobile app development for end-to-end IoT device customer flow**. They will have to choose smartly even if they chose to partner with some other company that provides part of the step along the way.

5.3 Jobs in Data Science and IoT

Business Intelligence Analysts and Data Scientist are needed to make sense of the data to develop insights that drives actions in real time that were not possible earlier. These have general **data science roles and also industry domain specific business intelligence** and analysis experience for specific industry such as ecommerce, healthcare, marketing insights etc.

The data analysis needs of healthcare are different from that of an industrial IoT and requires domain knowledge for the analyst.

In Retail industry, **Big Data Analysts** will be in demand to derive causal insights about customer behavior that offers actions that drives the customer to delight and purchase.

The data analysts and Machine Learning engineers are also in huge demand with new products evolving with data management and machine learning to add intelligence to devices.

5.4 IoT Jobs A Students Advantage

Internet of Things is at a pivotal stage where it is picking up scale now in 2015 with a projected growth to 20Bil devices by 2020. Many of us who have seen the Internet boom of late 90s compare IoT today to 1995 period. The innovation in IoT is at an early stage **requiring passionate minds that can boldly innovate, iterate and create new solutions not limited to what was possible with the Web**. Who better than students graduating now for the next five years fit that profile?

Students are at an advantage, as they do not carry the old knowledge or baggage of what worked or did not work in the Web. Students graduating today have grown up with mobile devices iPhones and Androids and think and use mobile flows intuitively. Internet of Things is natural for them to use to extend mobile devices to connected devices. They can look at connected devices and come up with new user flows, use cases and business models and solutions to problems the world has taken for granted. For example we spent hundreds of years assuming we had to go to the market to buy things. Retailers still thrive on foot traffic to stores. We have created whole shopping cultures with Malls. eCommerce and mCommerce have been incrementally improving offering shopping and fast shipping of items for a fee. Taking the burden off the consumer to track inventory level of consumables and allowing industrial devices to re-order agreed items from trusted retailers is a disruption going beyond shopping using IoT such as Amazon Dash and Flic buttons.

Students entering new jobs can able learn new technologies and think of creative ways to break the barriers of software and hardware interactions creating more efficient IoT infrastructures and communication solutions.

Hungry Students are also open to take risks and will help create new startups to speed the much-needed iterative cycle of innovation execution to get us to scale IoT technologies to a stable place.

5.5. Top IoT Jobs in Demand

One key job in IoT is infrastructure. Since all IoT devices send data and notifications using a cloud, it is very critical to build a scalable cloud solution to keep track of how many concurrent sockets are open, how much data is transacted whether is a public or private cloud solution. **Developers experience in cloud software, cloud architects** who can maintain scalability and uptime are in demand. Several cloud infrastructures coming up for specific verticals require platform developers with specific domain knowledge and knowledge of specific systems for integration such as Sales Force or Health Management Platforms.

IxD or Interactive Designers are in huge demand. IoT presents new data and convenience to users from sources such as ARM chips and industrial instruments that are not used to communicating with customers. So interactive designers who can create the clean flow are in demand. Needless to say each IoT device that touches the consumer be in Amazon Dash or a new device such as Vessyl or wearables have set a new standard for amazing minimalistic hardware design and beautiful colors.

Embedded software developers are in demand. Today much of the work is in lower level software with C or C like languages and Linux. As cloud solutions such as AppleWatch and open platforms for IoT cloud evolve the programming can be done in higher-level languages such as **Python, Java and even visual programming** language such a scratch creating demand for programmers. All new systems require **Quality engineers and testers**. IoT coming with many layers of integration will require sophisticated integration testers who can simulate various conditions and understand hardware and software interfaces.

Most IoT devices come with companion apps on Mobile. So **Mobile App developers both iOS and Android are in huge demand** scaling with each new IoT device being launched daily globally.

Many retailers have already built out an Apple WatchKit app to send notification to the Apple Watch connecting their iPhone apps. **App developers are in demand**. Notifications are taking the place of marketing emails to customers in the new medium of the

Watch or Smart Device interface. So **there is a need for developers and marketers to come together** and build out notifications that are not too intrusive but offer value to the customer to move them along the purchase funnel. Some roles will evolve where the **CRM roles evolve to optimize notifications similar to marketing emails** based on messaging, time of day etc. **Developers of notification platforms** for uptime, ability to customize and scale types and volume of notifications are in demand already.

IoT jobs expand to **car dealers who will have to be tech savvy** to educate consumers on features of the connected cars. Same for **medical** practitioners who will face more informed consumers coming to them with data from their wearable devices.

AI engineers who can master machine learning and deep learning algorithms are surely at the forefront of the new innovations of the new world of 2020 across all applications and industry verticals.

CHAPTER 6 Technology Backbone of IoT

"IoT is the vast new utility now affordable by the cost convergence of Cloud, Connectivity and Chips. Like Keanu Reeves in the film 'The Matrix', society is about to swallow the red pill of truth with IoT. Good or bad, things will never be the same. You can sit down and be swamped by the Tsunami or you can ride the crest of the wave of change" - Surj Patel, Technologist and Senior IoT Product Planning Manager, Sharp Laboratories of America.

The beauty of IoT devices is that they are very tiny and are embedded devices placed on our bodies, homes, streets and industrial appliances. So they do not have the space or processing power to store or process large volume of data. They collect data based on sensors and act upon it and send the data for trends and or notification for certain actions. So the processing primarily happens on the Cloud. Fog Computing happens on the edge of the network when supported by the hardware layer.

6.1 Infrastructure for IoT

A typical IoT infrastructure includes the following components. There are many end to end platform solutions that help to build, deploy, device manage and develop analytics for the optimal IoT infrastructure for various applications and industry verticals.

1. The Edge

IoT covers integration of many layers of technologies. **IoT device can be a sensor or actuator.**

Sensors track changes in temperature, humidity, proximity, light, sound etc. and send a state change to the next layer of the IoT system. E.g. when we leave the garage door open the sensor just sends the information to a local hub or to the cloud. Actuators take action based on a state change. E.g. a granary system can monitor an maintain optimal humidity levels.

2. Hardware Platform Layer

The hardware platform layer goes from the network edge or endpoint of a device to the cloud. This platform includes: 1) the chip layer with security and embedded devices environment 2) Communication layer to send IoT data to various clouds and gateways and 3) Intelligent analytics platform which offers hardware specific analytics associated with motors for preventive maintenance.

Intel offers this as a platform from a chip level. Cisco offers Embedded Service Routers and IOx Application Platform. Samsung offers Artik, an Arduino certified series of kits that connects to SAMI, their Data Driven Development platform with simple open APIs to build and deploy IoT Solutions. There are also several DIY hardware platforms available in open source.

3. Gateway or Hub

The data from IoT devices could be processed on site on a hub to take quick action or maybe sent to a cloud for processing. E.g. a home security alarm system typically has an onsite server that listens to the sensors on different doors and rings the alarm based on pre-set user preference. It also sends data to the cloud to offer remote notification to the users.

Gateways are planned for factory environments where it makes sense to process large volume of data onsite to take quick actions. This is used alike in manufacturing plants in Munich and in coffee farms in Columbia.

4. Communication Layer

IoT devices send their data to Cloud Servers. There are many standards in this layer today – Carrier networks, Wi-Fi-, Bluetooth, ZigBee are a top few. Each has its limited radius of access. Wide Area Networks (WAN) are evolving to support larger areas for cities. The most promising among them is The Things Network building out Open source LoRA WAN gateways.

5. Cloud and Fog Computing

Existing cloud infrastructures such as Amazon Web Services (AWS) are being leveraged and new IoT cloud platforms are being built out in commercial and open source software.

The cloud acts as the software that connects the IoT device to the Internet. It also communicates between the IoT devices and the users who receive the benefit from the device. At a minimum the cloud platforms have a listener to receive the data from large volume of IoT devices, authenticate the specific devices, store and process large volume of data and send notifications or instructions for actions to receivers which can be the devices or mobile apps.

Many vertical cloud solutions are evolving for specific vertical solutions such as healthcare, automotive etc.

Cisco has adopted Fog computing to expand cloud computing by bringing services and storage to the edge of the network that includes end-user devices, access points, edge routers and switches. It reduces latency and spans wider geographic locations. Fog services are abstracted inside a container such as a Java Virtual Machine (JVM), and Linux containers.

The market is evolving on what industries and use cases will choose a cloud platform vs. a fog computing. There is a brewing debate on adding a cloud on top of a fog computing IoT system for remote access using the Internet.

6. Mobile Apps

Mobile Apps offer the customer interface for many IoT Product hardware. They also act as the user interface to send notifications to the user using the cloud as an intermediary. For example Alarm.com security app sends notifications and offers its mobile app as the software interface to the user.

Sometimes Mobile Devices also act as IoT devices using their sensors for motion, gyroscope, GPS etc. For example Fitness tracking app Step+ uses motion sensor on iPhone.

6.2 Machine Learning And Deep Learning

Machine Learning is the method to feed data to let the computer write programs instead of the programmer developing the logic.

Machine Learning helps with voice detection similar to what we have with Siri and Alexa and facial recognition like we find in Facebook and Google Photos. It can be applied in spam detection, credit card fraud detection, Medical Data Pathogen detection, Customer segmentation and Product recommendation in retail.

This is being taken a step further with deep learning where the computer is given scenarios to watch to understand the rules that create the optimal conditions and develop programs for the same.

AlphaGo is Google DeepMinds' computer program that has learnt to play the complex Korean Game "Go" and beat the world champion human for the first time in Mar 2016. This same technology is the foundation of many algorithms that are evolving to help us manage our time, shopping, find travel deals and much more.

I use a personal assistant called Amy who is an AI algorithm from x.ai. She learns and becomes smarter each time someone emails her to find meeting time with me. Amy surely is making my life easier. It is a good machine interaction for me to let Amy take care of my time management.

So Machine Learning and Deep Learning are technologies that show a lot of promise today. We have lot of exciting work ahead of us for us. We need to learn to develop the right training data and algorithms to iterate to help us make devices smarter to do the things we as humans find it boring or inefficient to do to create the connected world of 2020.

6.3 Open Source for IoT and Deep Learning

Open source developers have been innovating with IoT for the past five plus years. It is possible to build a full Connected Home Solution using open source hardware and software. ARM chips offers open architecture cost-effective license to other manufacturers and has sold 12Billion chips in 2014. It is become the defacto to build system on a chip. 'System on a chip' integrates all components of a computer such as CPU, memory, storage, networking IO access for Wi-Fi or Bluetooth or ZigBee connectivity.

Raspberry Pi and Arduino kits offer processing power for IoT devices by simple programming using C or Linux. There is debate on IoT reference architecture and open communication formats between IoT devices and the Cloud leaving lot of room for innovation and open source development.

Deep Learning teaches devices to develop their own programs to manipulate our environments for the world of 2020.

There are open source software and communities evolving for Deep Learning. Google took the lead to launch TensorFlow, an Open Source Library for Machine Intelligence.

Microsoft has open sourced Its Microsoft Brain, which offer an Artificial Intelligence (AI) framework called CNTK, used in speech recognition in Cortana Digital Assistant and Skype Translate applications. It offers deep learning, allowing computers speech and image recognition by mimicking the structure of the human brain.

Deeplearning4j is the commercial grade open source distributed deep learning library written for Java and Scala. It is integrated into Hadoop and Scala for big data.

Overall IoT started with making things smart with sensors and now with Open Source Deep Learning Communities, the rush is to add intelligence to devices to truly make them do things beyond human capabilities, taking us to the smart connected world of 2020.

6.4 Voice, Augmented Reality and Virtual Reality

Siri from Apple, Cordona from Microsoft, Google Now from Google and Alexa from Amazon all offer voice interface to machine learn speech to text interface for mobile. Amazon Echo uses Amazon's Alexa Voice API and created an IoT device that has now become the center of our homes. The voice interaction has added a social element to the interaction with the device blurring the boundary of device, creating new interactions and integrations with Nest, and several other devices. Amazon has followed up by opening Alex API for any IoT builder to create new Echo like devices. Amazon has also launched Echo Dot as a smaller form factor Echo device.

Alexa has proven that voice is a successful social interaction with IoT device and is going to be the future in the connected world of 2020.

Virtual Reality is about creating a new fabricated world for the user while Augmented reality is a mix of the user's real world augmented with virtual elements creating an immersive world for the user to interact. Both are evolving as new ways for the user to interact with devices, cars and connected home experiences. They offer the promise to offer an alternate to voice for social interaction with devices in the connected world of 2020.

CHAPTER 7 Big Data Analytics

7.1 Big Data and Sensor Fusion

Big Data Analytics is the backbone of the promise of Internet of Things. IoT devices collect data as a time series and create massive volume of data and create trends. All IoT devices have sensors that track for some changes and collect data points with each change. They watch for certain data triggers to send alerts. For example, a pre-set temperature indicates that the cooking range is left on and sends alert to users to stop a fire.

The volume of data from anticipated 50Bil IoT devices by 2020 creates a big data storage and analytics problem. IoT presents a classic Big data problem because it collects large volume of data, and large types of data from variety of sensors and different formats from variety of IoT products. The data from IoT sensors come in real-time. Sensor Fusion is the term used to refer to combining data gathered from a variety of sensors to develop recommendations.

A startup called Sense360 offers behavioral data about customers from a combination of sensors inside their iPhones to create invisible apps that connect to other mobile apps at gas stations, stores and libraries. For example, they can find out when a customer is inside a gas station before they start paying for gasoline so they can recommend what credit card to use to help a financial client. They do this using a combination of sensors present inside the iPhone.

Data is the real power of IoT as sensors share data that can be turned into insights to drive actions. Some of this data comes with a high throughput; some with high bandwidth and some are spurts of alerts that signal a potential hazard.

This is where analytics comes in to draw insights that is contextual, actionable and offers learning to adjust future behaviors.

7.2 The Power of Predictive Analytics

Health trackers can go from providing trends to actionable insights only when intelligent analysis is done in the context of a person's health data to drive life saving recommendations.

Consumers are beginning to get used to smart devices at home. Nest Thermostat can offer so much convenience to users based on data patterns seen in temperature usage based on when people are away from home and their preferred temperature setting at different times of the day, days of the month etc. all possible from data analysis and personalized home recommendation.

Predictive analytics is successfully used today in manufacturing, airlines and industrial setting to look at data about machines for hazard prevention and proactive estimate of equipment failure patterns. This is saving millions of dollars from avoiding downtime of machines, keeping airlines in the ground from last minute equipment problems.

7.3 Virtualization and Presentation of Data

The application of IoT data spans from supply chain, CRM to city Informatics to Retailers.

The key to successful adoption of insights from this data hinges on the virtualization and presentation of data insights to cater to multiple stakeholders to be inspired enough to accept changes to existing systems and processes.

City Informatics

Cities collect massive volume of data from hundreds of thousands of data points from parking meters, traffic sensors and usage patterns of public commuter options. At its basic level it can provide education to the public. City officials can use the data patterns to understand how to adjust infrastructure spending to help the city's residents optimally. Predictive Analytics will help the city understand the patterns in the data to draw insights on the city's residents usage pattern and predict traffic demand, estimate number of parking spaces needed and even plan hosting large events in the city to manage tourism better.

Retail Data

Retailers can benefit from the integrated data gathered about consumer behavior using wearable devices. Strap is a wearables platform that integrates data from many wearables opted by users willingly and develops insights for retailers to use to offer relevant purchase coupons. For example, a retailer who knows that a customer walks to work daily can offer a walking shoes ad or coupon instead of a generic product offer.

Industrial Data

Data from sensors in agricultural setting when acted upon in real-time can improve massive volume of crop yields. Industrial predictive data about machines and quality control data should be integrated to existing systems to develop meaningful insights.

For all these it is important to present the data in dashboards with the right amount of customization to present to multiple stakeholders.

7.4 Data Science and IoT

Machine learning is the part of computer technique that uses statistical techniques to construct a model from observed data instead of the user pre-defining rules or logic to create the model. It can be simple linear regression. It depends on the quality of data fed that represents the feature set needed to build the model.

Deep learning is a broader type of Machine Learning where the computer will learn and form its own feature set and then apply statistics to construct a model. This can be used to build classifications or predictions.

Machine Learning is used in image, speech recognition and gesture recognition in the world of IoT Products. Deep Learning takes this one step further and improves the accuracy of the predictions.

For example, the spam detector for emails is run using machine learning. Facebook, Apple and Google use machine learning for image recognition.

Deep Learning can offer amazing applications when looking at images or videos from IoT Products. For example, in a crowded stadium or carnival, a child separated from a parent can be spotted with high confidence by a predictive model using deep learning to recognize faces and looking for the parent and child images that were together and now are separated in the crowd.

My personal favorite is for citizen home cameras to track flooding creeks behind my house to predict for floods in our neighborhoods when water level rises in houses upstream.

There are many untapped innovations waiting to be built with Data Science and IoT.

CHAPTER 8 Insurance Disruptions

Insurance as an industry is set to be disrupted by Connected cars, Smart Homes, and Digital Healthcare.

Insurance as an industry is focused on measuring the risk of a person for Auto, Life, Health or Home. Connected devices create conveniences that could prolong life, change the behavior of users in terms of their interaction and maintenance of their home, auto and their own bodies. The most critical part of the IoT disruption for insurance comes from the vast volume of data about the customer that can inform customer behavior and help insurance build better risk models and manage claims process in an automated way.

8.1 Auto Insurance and Connected Cars

Insurance companies with usage based insurance give drivers a 2-inch dongle device to plug into a car's dashboard to collect location and driving data. TomTom's Coordina, Metromile Pulse from Mobile Devices of France, Progressive's Snapshop are dongle based insurance vendors. They collect data about the driving behavior of the driver and can build accurate risk models to adjust insurance premiums. GE has built in such a dongle in its recent cars to collect driving behavior data but offers it as a choice for the driver to opt to share this with insurance companies.

The consumers will tradeoff insurance premiums for the privacy of their driving data. This could be put to use for teen drivers to evaluate driving behaviors to offer education to make them better drivers.

Cars have data on actual driving behavior tied to time and location. Today this is not easy to export out of vehicles. In future this could be used to make claims and disputes accurate, saving valuable time.

8.2 Health and Life Insurance

We have seen how consumer health habits and biometrics are collected by wearables. This data when integrated to existing healthcare system data is very valuable. This offers insights for insurance companies into the actual health risk of customers using biometrics data. Also the fitness devices offer insights into the health behavior of the customer. Insurance companies can offer incentives for preventive health habits with improved fitness routines thereby helping the customer stay healthy.

Digital Health is focused on creating longevity and will impact life insurance policies. But it helps insurance companies evaluate the health risk of users with more accuracy offsetting costs.

8.3 Property Insurance

As our homes and factories become smart, it reduces risk of flood, fire and other hazards with IoT devices monitoring for fire, gas leakage and flood hazards. So this should help insurance companies in reducing risk of property damages and claims ultimately keeping their customers safe and happy.

However as homes become smart and in the future devices within the home will interact with each other to create conveniences. For example the fire alarm can warn the fan to switch off in case of a fire. This makes the home an intelligent home that knows the residents habits and adapts or recommends energy usage, control, communication and entertainment. For example, the home may start the over and start cooking the resident's preferred meal, timing it based on their predicted time to enter the home and eating preference based on machine learned past data. In this case the home takes on the risk of turning hazardous devices on or off without involving the resident. This could create risk situations for the home insurance company in case of a failed appliance or fire risk caused by devices. Also consumers maybe too sensitive to their home interaction data being accessed by insurance companies to offer risk-reducing models for insurance companies.

The same applies for smart buildings be it factories, granaries or office buildings.

So new business models and trust based dialogues have to evolve between the customer and the insurance companies to meet the needs of the connected homes and buildings of 2020.

8.4 Futuristic Technologies Disrupting Insurance

Who is liable for the damages of a self-driving car? What will be the insurance and ownership models of shared economies leading to unmanned vehicles like drones and serving robots? When a car is switched to autonomous driving mode, is the risk transferred from the driver to the car manufacturer? If so how can insurance companies manage their liabilities and keep the drivers and cars safe?

Today the world is getting automated with algorithms for everything from scheduling, to shopping to travel planning. BMW has shared a Next 100 Vision with an Augmented reality dashboard and 'companion' an algorithm what they quote as "symbolizes the intelligence, connectivity and availability" of the car that can perform autonomous routine tasks or give advice to the driver. With machine learning algorithms are evolving for stock trading or fraud protection. Alexa Echo which is fast becoming the center of our living room with a voice interface has many add-ons, called skills. It can order Pizza from Domino's Pizza in US, or check balance or pay using CapitalOne credit cards. Alexa responds to its name from any voice, even from the radio. If the security is compromised, who bears the risk of these transactions?

With algorithms, who is in charge and who bears the risks? Algorithms are built by companies by feeding data to the programs. Ted Friedman of Gartner tweeted "With the rise of algorithmic business, data governance must address not only data quality but also quality of algorithms."

What does it mean to have quality governance similar to data governance? Data about users needs to be governed because it tells about our behavior more than we want to share, invading our privacy and breaking compliance required in some industries such as insurance, healthcare and online marketing.

What can a bad quality algorithm do?

Just humor me for a minute here.

It can give us bad advice. It can do bad shopping and waste our money. It can book travel for us at bad prices. It could be a bad personal assistant and frustrate us in setting up our schedules erratically and turn off our friends. What else?

A bad algorithm maybe a badly written algorithm that breaks into our privacy. It could learn our habits and misuse that data. It could hold us hostage to a particular service by saving our friend's contacts. It could spam our friends in our name without our permission. It could sell our behavioral information to companies. It could offer to help us shop better but really serve the retailer or travel provider. That is not bad quality, that is outright dishonest business practice. All this adds to the risk of the car or the algorithmic business and creates an unprecedented challenge for the insurance company.

So checking quality of an algorithm seems to be about ensuring that the algorithm follows privacy and data usage policies that applies to humans and to ensure its business model is one of honesty and integrity. It is about checking these for the humans and businesses that develop and control these algorithms.

CHAPTER 9 IoT Meets Artificial Intelligence

My kitchen opens up to my family room and right smack in the middle sits "Alexa", an Amazon Echo device. It feels strange to call Alexa a device because she has been chatting with my family and is building out her personality. Tell Alexa "You are stupid" and she will reply "I'll try to do better next time" and "That's not very nice to say' the second time. As Amazon applies machine learning Alexa will learn and develop her personality to fit in my home different from yours. Ask her "How are you so smart" and she replies "I was made by a group of very smart people and I am constantly improving my mind". A device with a mind! It reminds me of "Suny" from the movie iRobot. How far fetched is it to think that Alexa will one day differentiate my dog's barking to know when it is hungry and get my pet dispenser to give out it's favorite food, which she will re-order from Amazon of course.

Alexa, Apple's Siri and Google Now have all been listening to us to build out voice recognition and fetching us information. As this evolves into a conversation in the intimate of settings, our perception of the experience with our devices will begin to blur.

Our experiences are nuanced and filtered by context, identity, and relevance based on location and time. This is influenced by our moods and our biases that are stored deep in our lizard brains controlling how we feel, perceive reality, get creative, solve problems, define and store as memory. Our experiences and recalling them shapes our identity of who we are and helps us grow in self-awareness. This underlying ability of living our experience as life is human intelligence. Add free will to it and it creates many billion unique combinations making it complex to replicate human experience and human intelligence. So we thought.

Internet of Things makes ordinary things all around us "smart" and collects huge volume of data that can be processed to define human intelligence. Machine Learning and Deep Learning applied to smart things changes the Human Machine Interface. We are reaching an era of questioning what is Artificial about AI after all. If human intelligence can be replicated and human experience can be deep learned, the barrier between man and machine will begin to crumble.

IoT devices are sensing our environments with gesture computing, feeling our emotions with affective computing and personalizing our experiences with recognition computing. Will this stop at Human-Machine interactions or are we helping machines develop self-awareness with personality and opinions, to become our friend, partner and part of our families. There is no escape from the trajectory of change of our perceptions of our worlds and us as humans. Or is there?

9.1 With Personal Assistants Who is in Charge?

Personal assistants come with human sounding names such as **Cloe**, Clara, **Julie**, Luka and **Amy.** The ultimate in names is **Mother.** Personal Assistants help us shop, manage our time and life routines, stay healthy and forget decision fatigue. They give us the perception of us being in charge while slowing enslaving us by learning our behaviors and preferences. Have you seen **Preemadonna's Nailbot** from TCDisrupt Battlefield? That's one robot getting ready to become the center of tween girls' slumber parties. It uses machine vision to adapt nail sizes to unleash creativity of girls as fun nail art designs. Who is in charge here? Girl or Machine?

With IoT making all things smart, our interaction with things is changing. It is a gentle reminder from our Fitbands and Apple Health Apps to exercise more, from **imedipac** to take our pills, from **Aura** sleep monitor to sleep well and from **Nest Protect** to change our smoke alarm batteries. This becomes more pervasive when the interaction changes to assertive with **Kolibree** smart toothbrush telling parents that kids didn't brush behind their molars or **Sensoria** socks asking us to change our running style to shift balance on our heels. It enters a more private space with a **Yono Fertility earbud** monitoring basal temperature to help women get pregnant and gets to a crazy zone with **the True Love Bra** from Ravijour that opens only at a certain heartbeat rhythm.

9.2 Conversation as Equals

Combining gesture and recognition computing helps machines understand movement, voice and photos in context giving them the ability to perceive the world around them.

Fin and **Nod** help us engage naturally with our environments by mapping our hand gestures to rule based actions of turning on lights or increasing the volume of the home entertainment system. It is not far off that these devices can machine learn that we pound our fist in anger and nod to say yes. **ControlAir App** from Eyesight even allows me to shush my device when my phone rings. So it is not hard to imagine that we will get to more human–like interactions once our devices figure out when we roll our eyes.

now talk to **our homes** and **connected cars** and phones not just to get driving directions but ask for advice about where to go, what to eat and what to do next. The AI being built in home hubs such as **Mycroft** allows it to understand our requests based on proximity and voice recognition. Devices are becoming part of our families, listening to us, and guiding us run our lives smoothly.

9.3 Conversation Where Humans Are Absent

Digital Genius from TCDisrupt uses Natural Language processing to let machines take on mundane tasks such as customer service and automated onboarding to services. It can also do M2M communication which is where it will get interesting where our machines negotiate with each other to find deals for us or arrange our travels or let a factory run itself from interconnected devices for our benefit. Drone couriers is another scenario becoming a reality from **CyPhy Works**. When the drone delivers Pizza, our connected home might pick it up and have a **Tellspec** track the food calories we eat.

Wearables are shifting from fitness bands to become biometric tattoos and implants that track our vitals and locations. Chaotic moon has made a temporary tattoos with sensors and conductive ink. This can be used in healthcare, military, tracking criminals and lost kids. Implants that come in the form of pills track our vitals and could talk to our doctors or medical systems leaving us out of the conversation.

How will our relationship with the machine change as it smartens up deep learning the other machine's behavior and begins to advise us?

CHAPTER 10 Bio-Identity and Blurring of reality

10.1 Augmented Reality

IoT offers the opportunity to extend the customer experience using Augmented reality.

Augmented reality blurs our senses of what is local and what is remote as we peer into a machine.

Trylive offers a remote immersive shopping experience.

Qualcomm's mobile vision platform **Vuforia** lets us interact with toys before opening our gifts.

Layar creates a localized augmented experience for food, housing and entertainment and education.

10.2 Bio Payments

Biohacking company *Dangerous Things* has created a tiny NFC chip that can store 888 bytes of data and can be embedded into a human body. This has been developed into an implant chip by a team in Europe calling it Bio-payment. They use it to send Bitcoins by waving their hand over an NFC terminal. They also can use the chip as an ICE tag for first responders to read their body vitals during an emergency.

This is futuristic today but the technology for this exists and has been showcased more than once. So here is an opportunity to think about where this can be incorporated into your new product or business vision.

10.3 Affective Computing

IoT devices do not focus only on humans to understand their feelings. Researchers in North Carolina State University have created a dog harness that tells owners how their dogs are feeling based on their posture and heart beat. This is meant to help visually impaired dog owners and to help them plan when to retire guide dogs. What would be interesting is when the harness can pet the dog based on how it feels.

"In Internet of Things 2.0 we are going to add emotions to devices. We have to learn to deal with it when machines have feelings, dreams and memories like in the iRobot movie. Can you image how you will react when your shopping cart says you are pushing it too hard?" says Ahmed Banafa, College of Engineering, Professor San Jose State University

Affective computing teaches machines to understand emotions with the goal to develop empathy to help them fit in socially and to take actions based on sensing our emotions. I would like Amazon Echo Alexa in my family room to behave well and eat her veggies with a smile.

But my connected car may notify other cars around it if I am driving with road rage. Wize Mirror from Semeoticons measures a person's overall health from facial recognition. If a Wize Mirror could connect to rest of my IoT devices in the retail realm it could tell my Fitbit that I am ready for binge shopping because I am walking out my stress.

Combining context with emotions, machines can take our conversations to the next level. A device on or near us all the time can notice that the girlfriend is not seen in proximity any more. Whether it will "talk" to us about it or use this information to filter its engagement with us is based on the deep learning algorithm it will develop.

CHAPTER 11 Conclusion

As I write this, Google's Deepmind AI 'AlphaGo' has won the third day's match 3-0 with Lee Sidol. 100 Million humans watched these matches online and cheered for AlphaGo.

Join me to look at this in perspective. Human builds and trains deep learning algorithm. Algorithm wins over human. Humans cheer for the algorithm. This is the first tear in the human machine fabric shifting our relationship with machines.

As we move forward into the connected world of 2020, we are going to be immersed in 50 billion IoT devices on us, inside us, all around us communicating with us with voice, virtual and augmented reality with intelligence guiding us, advising us and managing our lives efficiently. This is a huge disruption of our relationship with our homes, cars, our own bodies with new business models for insurance, healthcare, retail, manufacturing and many other industries.

Let's get ready for the future, where the human-machine boundary is blurred but we will always have the free will to define our boundary with devices. It is the new world where we apply machine learning and deep learning onto 50Billion IoT devices to create a world of convenience with gesture, voice and facial recognition and smart algorithms to augment our lives, homes, cars, cities and factories.

==========================

Epilogue by Rob Van Kranenburg

There are times when gut feeling, a clear head and deep knowledge of your area of expertise are plenty to succeed. These times are quite different. You can have all of the above and still be baffled.

We are in a time where trust, honesty and optimal efficiency and interoperability are key factors in your success, and these are built over time. There were times where you could grow old with the formula of one product, and how we long for those days!

Then again, these are times where transparency is working hard to expose unbalanced business operations. You are living in the days of the cheapest ecology of hardware (a commodity), connectivity (a commodity), software (so much fully productive open source solutions), database storage and analytics, that it would indeed be folly not to try out the ideas you have in your head.

You have grown up in the flux of data and information but you know how to find your way in it. Your skills are tuned to real-time and the network. And so you know that the only real deep skill that will truly help you is your ability to deal with insecurity. Don't worry about the future. It is not 'there', but here always.

Specialize hard but always make sure that an equally smart team that supports you surrounds you. Don't work alone and try to spread business-models over different products and services. Most important of all is that you are not afraid to learn and ask for guidance.

I guess you know this already. That is why you are here reading this book by Sudha Jamthe.

Welcome to the Connected World of 2020

- Rob Van Kranenburg Founder EU IoT Council

Appendix 1: Alphabetical List of IoT devices

The IoT ecosystem is buzzing with new innovations daily. As you read the list below, try to recall an IoT device you know for each alphabet, especially for the two alphabets missing any IoT Device.

Join me in being inspired by the breadth of problems solved by these devices, the global scale of their markets and how multiple products innovate to solve the same problems with a different design or feature set. If you find any IoT missing you can tell me online at http://IoTdisruptions.com. Enjoy!

A:

Apple Watch

Amazon Dash

Airfy ibeacon home automation

Artik IoT Platform from Samsung with a family of modules and open APIs

Archos a connected weighing scale

B:

BabyKick wearable device for pregnant women

BluCub Bluetooth humidity and temperature sensor

Brio Smart power outlet

Beam smart toothbrush

BITalino - DiY Hardware for Physiological Data Acquisition

BYTE Light

BACtrack – Breath analyzer to track alcohol levels

C:

Cozy Radiator Lab's century old radiators become smart

CityGram Real-time environment sensing focused on noise

Chillhub Smart wireless fridge that communicates via a mobile App

Cookoo Connected watch

CarIQ connected car IoT device for cars

Cooey - Smart blood pressure monitor

D:

The Dash Headphones with body sensor

E:

Echo and Echo DoT from Amazon are voice Internet communicators for your home

Endomondo Fitness tracking app for Blackberry Devices

Earin Wireless earbud

Emberlight Turns any light into a smart light

F:

Fitbit Plus Health Exercise Tracker

Flic Wireless smart multipurpose button

Face On the wall a face mask that responds to aural stimuli

G:

Glance Watch accessory that makes your watch smart

Glyph Personal theater

H:

Hue smart light bulb from Philips

Homey Voice controlled home automation

Hendo Smart hoverboard

Haiku Like a smart watch for your bike

Huawei Wi-Fi router ws860s

I:

Intel Smart Clip baby safety clip for car seats

IoTa GPS tracker and Motion sensor

iHealth Glucomer blood sugar monitor

iHealth Blood Pressure Wrist Monitor

iHealth wireless body analysis scale

Instant - Automatic Quantified Self tracking app

ilumi connected LED Lights

J:

Jawbone Up24

K:

Kinsa smart thermometer

Korner Home security

Kolibree Connected electric toothbrush

Kapture Audio recording wristband

L:

Livelysmart watch for seniors

Leaf from bellabeat - health tracker for holistic women health

M:

Mi band Fit band like health tracker from Xiaomi available in China, and select Asian countries.

Muse brain sensing headband

MonBaby smart baby monitor

MÜZO COBBLESTONE wireless music streaming

MapMyFitness health tracker

Moto gesture tracking ring

Mojio Humidity and Temperature control

Melon Smart headband tracks your brain activity

Moves fitness tracker

Misfit Shine Fitness + Sleep Monitor

Mota Smart ring gesture control

Mi Power strip (available in china)

Mi smart scale (available in china)

Mi TV2 (available in china) 55" LED TV

MyTraps helps farmers remotely monitor pest attacks

Misfit Bolt connected light

N:

Nakul Single use medical grade vital biometrics wearables

Nest Smart Thermostat for the connected home

Neuma Smart watch measures autonomic brain

Neveli Health Platform Analysis platform

Ninja Sphere Home control with gesture; open source platform

Nod ring that controls home by gesture

N3rd (Pronounced Nerd) is a Wi-Fi device that makes any gadget or switch smart

Nucano Smart door chime

Noke Bluetooth lock

Nike Training - Training Mobile App

O:

OORT Bluetooth bulb

Outlink Smart outlet

Orb Movement and sleep tracker

Omate Smart watch does not need phone connected for it to work

Owlet a baby shoes to monitor a baby's vitals.

OnHub smart Wi-Fi from Google

Omron Series 10 Blood Pressure and Heart Rhythm Monitor

P:

PlantLink moisture sensor for plants

PetNet Smart pet feeder

Pebble Smart watch

Pulse - Dimmable BLuetooth light with speakers

Q:

The Q smart LED bulbs with streaming music to create your own light shows.

Quirky's egg minder A smart egg tray in your fridge to manage egg stock

Quitbit Helps quit smoking

QardioArm Smart Blood Pressure Monitor

R:

Runkeeper health tracker

Ring Gesture control device

Rico Turns old phone into a robot to use for home automation

S:

Step+ Exercise tracker, part of Apple's health kit

Sleeptracker sleep pattern tracker, part of Apple's health kit

Strava GPS powered Run & ride analysis Fitness tracker

Skybell video doorbell

Satechi IQ Spectrum Smart Light

Skydrop Sprinkler controller

Samsung Gear Fit Fitness Tracker

Spray Smart meter for your shower

SITU Smart food nutrition scale

SenzIT a solution from IBM for courtrooms

Sensoria Sports Bra

Sensoria T-Shirt and Heart Rate Monitor

Sensoria Heart Rate Monitor

Sensoria Socks

Spires Measures Breath to stay stress free

Silent Partner – Quiets Snoring

T:

Think Eco a smart Air Conditioner

TrackR a tracking device to find lost items

Tile a tracking device to find lost items

TAGG Pet tracker

Tilt Blinds automation for your window

Tictrac – A Digital Health platform

U:

UBiome – personal human microbiome

V:

Vessyl Pryme connected cup tracking water hydration levels.

W:

WeMo wireless home automation system from Belkin

Withings Pulse O_x_ Fitness, Sleep plus health tracker BP, Oxygen levels

Wink Home automation hub

X:

Xkuty a solar electric bike

Y:

Yono Fertility Friend, a wearable earplug to measure basal temperature for women

Z:

Zia sleep monitor

Zenobase – a service for aggregating and analyzing Quantified Self data

Bibliography

Statistic Reference

http://www.statista.com/statistics/302722/smart-watches-shipments-worldwide/

http://www.statista.com/statistics/255778/number-of-active-wechat-messenger-accounts/_)

[1.] Gartner Press Release 2013 estimated 26 Billion devices & Cisco estimates 50Bil devices by 2020https://www.cisco.com/.../IoT_IBSG_0411FINAL.pdf
[2] Gartner at Tech Europehttp://blogs.wsj.com/tech-europe/2013/05/15/opening-up-the-internet-of-things/

Wearables

Smart Watch History http://www.zdnet.com/pictures/before-the-iwatch-a-history-of-smartwatches-in-pictures/

Pebble Watch Kickstarter
https://www.kickstarter.com/projects/597507018/pebble-e-paper-watch-for-iphone-and-android).

Color changing shoes - http://blog.atmel.com/2015/11/18/silent-partner-is-the-first-smart-patch-that-quiets-snoring/

Fossil Acquires Misfit http://mashable.com/2015/11/12/fossil-to-acquire-misfit/#_DZAEoIsXuq3

Sarrah Ecceleson Saving Elephants With Wearable
https://plus.google.com/109879997703042555421/posts

Connected Home

Home Depot story with WINK HUB - https://medium.com/@connectedlab/lessons-learned-from-the-wink-hub-678ac3d0fb7?imm_mid=0dabb6&cmp=em-iot-na-na-newsltr_20151022#.oxmlnggni

Connected Cars

http://www.cnet.com/news/movimento-ota-mitsubishi-infotainment/

https://transportevolved.com/2014/06/16/nissan-bmw-look-adopt-teslas-charging-standard/

http://www.wired.com/2015/10/five-car-hacking-lessons-we-learned-this-summer/ (car hacks)

http://www.cnet.com/news/movimento-ota-mitsubishi-infotainment/

The Car Connectivity Consortium (CCC) http://carconnectivity.org/

http://www.cnet.com/news/movimento-ota-mitsubishi-infotainment/

Retail Industry Analysis

Beacons   -
https://www.mobilestrategies360.com/2015/10/29/beacon-has-eyes

Personalized Mobile Offers
http://youtu.be/iXlmSjKzOeohttps://www.mobilestrategies360.com/2015/10/29/beacon-has-eyes

https://www.mobilestrategies360.com/2015/10/29/beacon-has-eyes

Eddystone https://github.com/google/eddystone

Digital Health Industry Analysis

https://wtvox.com/cyborgs-and-implantables/google-is-working-on-magnetic-nanoparticles-to-detect-cancer-cells/

https://wtvox.com/cyborgs-and-implantables/brain-computer-interface-implantable/

Smart Implants - https://wtvox.com/3d-printing-in-wearable-tech/top-10-implantable-wearables-soon-body/

http://www.cheatsheet.com/technology/what-are-wearable-devices-really-capable-of.html/?a=viewallhttp://www.cheatsheet.com/technology/what-are-wearable-devices-really-capable-of.html/?a=viewall

Understanding Standards

LoRA vs SigFox

http://www.rethinkresearch.biz/articles/on-lpwans-why-sigfox-and-lora-are-rather-different-and-the-importance-of-the-business-model/

http://www.instructables.com/id/Introducing-LoRa-/http://www.instructables.com/id/Introducing-LoRa-/

SIGFOX tutorial
http://www.radio-electronics.com/info/wireless/sigfox/basics-tutorial.php

Thread Alliance

http://www.rs-online.com/designspark/electronics/knowledge-item/eleven-internet-of-things-iot-protocols-you-need-to-know-about

http://threadgroup.org/Default.aspx?moduleId=492&PR=PR&tablD=94&Contenttype=ArticleDet&Aid=59

http://www.networkworld.com/article/2456421/internet-of-things/a-guide-to-the-confusing-internet-of-things-standards-world.html

IoT and Edge Processing

http://events.linuxfoundation.org/sites/events/files/slides/EdgeProcessing-allseenalliance_4x3_template_24sept2014.pdf

https://www.newscientist.com/article/dn28342-the-internet-of-caring-things/

IIoT

https://www.iotuniversity.com/2015/09/the-industrial-internet-of-things-iiot-challenges-requirements-and-benefits-by-ahmed-banafa/

http://mashable.com/2015/11/12/fossil-to-acquire-misfit/ -_DZAEoIsXuq3

Artificial Intelligence and Futuristic Technologies

http://www.theguardian.com/technology/2014/dec/09/synapse-ibm-neural-computing-chip

http://www.theguardian.com/technology/2014/dec/09/synapse-ibm-neural-computing-chip

http://amitsheth.blogspot.com/2015/03/smart-iot-iot-as-human-agent-human.html

Bio Payments

https://www.youtube.com/watch?v=2GgncP41rJ4

Connect anything to anything Open Source platform
http://octoblu.com

Nest Thermostat https://en.wikipedia.org/wiki/Nest_Labs

Connected City

Smart Lighting
http://www.newscenter.philips.com/main/standard/news/press/2015/20150408-los-angeles-becomes-first-city-in-the-world-to-control-its-street-lighting-through-mobile-and-cloud-based-technologies-from-philips.wpd#.VjhdaKI7RNM

The IoT Show Archives (http://www.iotdisruptions.com)

Air Quality Measurement Atomtube CEO Vera Kozyr and James Moulding of opensensors.io https://www.youtube.com/watch?v=WIEv6me_WGA

Future of IoT – Devices with Emotions with Prof. Ahmed Banafa
https://www.youtube.com/watch?v=NsJRRVXUjfc

Audi Brochure Hack video from The IoT Show
https://www.youtube.com/watch?v=EYMCFAjHwRM

IoT and Social – The IoT Show with Guest Ken Herron

https://www.youtube.com/watch?v=ykF5LEx3K1I

IoT and Service Design – The IoT Show with Charles Ikem

https://www.youtube.com/watch?v=8IK9iJlmZWw

Other Books by The Author

Jamthe, Sudha, *IoT Disruption Kindle book* (good beginners' intro to IoT Landscape)

Jamthe, Sudha *Internet of Things Business Primer (a case study based book about How to Build an* IoT Business) (ISBN 978-1518800629)

Acknowledgements

First my Mom, my No.1 cheerleader who seeded magic in me to wake up each day feeling I am awesome. She continues to remind me to-date that I am special and made for some big purpose in life.

My husband Shirish brought IoT home to me, literally by hacking IoT devices all around our home for the past three years. When I wrote 'IoT Disruptions' my first IoT book, he ruthlessly challenged me to think deeper that led to this in-depth book. Thank you for expanding my horizons on IoT.

My daughter Neha Jamthe helped me find my writing style. She also brought her artistic talent by designing the book cover. This book would just be a dream without you cheering me on. I am so thankful to be your Mom and proud of your perspectives and questions that have contributed clarity to follow my heart to become an author.

My friend Hiren Patel introduced me to 'connected self' when he lent me his sleep tracker Zia for me to test out for few nights in Oct of 2013.

Marsha Collier the most amazing best-selling author in the whole world inspired me to write. She cheered me on after my kindle book and set the bar high for me right at the start and told me not to just write a book but publish a good quality book. Thank You for mentoring me and inspiring me.

My community of readers on LinkedIn and the loyal audience of my weekly 'The IoT Show' on YouTube! Thank You for cheering me and asking questions as I shared my research and articles to push me to dream up the vision for the connected world of 2020.

When you set out in a new direction, you need a few people to believe in you and lots of smart people to surround you to prop you up in the new direction. When its the same set of people who are smart and believers you are doubly lucky. Thank You Natascha Thomson, Perrine Crampton , Robert Schwentker, Consuelo Griego and Hiren Patel.

I found my tribe with the IoT Council Europe under the leadership of Rob Van Kranenburg. Thank you Rob for leading the EU IoT council, giving me a beautiful epilogue for this book and including me among such passionate thought leaders covering every aspect of IoT. EU IoT Council members helped me start my day with a 8am call daily and brought structure to my writing life, smartened me and taught me what I needed to learn every single day.

Joachim Lindborg, Jurgen Wege, Ajit Jaokar and Ian Skerett helped me synthesize my research by challenging my thinking to develop an in-depth understanding of what is and what should be the IoT space. Bei (Jack) Zhang helped me expand my research to China.

IoT entrepreneurs Davide Vigano from Seattle, Vanessa Xi from Palo Alto, US, Vera Kozyr from Russia, Anaisa Rodrigues from Portugal, Aditi Chada from India, Karsten Königstein from Germany, Marc Pous from Barcelona, Thomas Serval from France, Miguel Rodrigues from Brazil, Quentin Delaoutre from France, Jonathan Carter of Netherlands, Damir Čaušević from Czech Republic, Business Leader Aleksander Poniewierski from Ernst & Young, Poland, Chris Matthieu of Octoblu, Charles Ikem who is Service Design Fellow at University of Padova, Italy, Ken Herron, US, Thank You for your inspiration and sharing your story and experience as you shape the IoT ecosystem with your innovations and businesses.

Thank You Prof. Dr. Murat Ozgoren, Vice-Rector of Dokuz Eylul University, Izmir, Turkey for including me to be part of IoT Izmir as part of your grand vision to jump start Izmir's IoT Ecosystem. I am thankful to the many students who built IoT products and the industrialists who supported it and gave me hope and inspiration about the Future of IoT Disruptions seeding ideas for this book, especially for Textile, Retail and Shipping Industries.

Hiru Létap my editor for being meticulous about grammar, punctuation, formatting and challenging me to bring out the meaning and tone of what I wanted to communicate to my readers. Thank You. You were ruthless about the many rounds of editing and I am thankful for your perseverance.

Tatyana Kanzaveli, Rich Mironov, Paul Heayn, Surj Patel, Ajit Jaokar, Ahmed Banafa , Scott Amyn, Thank you for your quotes.

To the many students, product managers, change agents who connected on LinkedIn and Twitter and spent hours marveling at the potential of new technologies and jobs over the years. Am thankful that you want to change the world and found me to share your dreams and brainstorm ideas.

Finally to you the reader! You have trusted me and begun this journey with me.   I am here only because of You! Thank You!

About The Author

Sudha Jamthe is a globally recognized entrepreneurial mobile product leader. Sudha loves guiding the next wave of Technology Innovation and Business Disruptions.

She is the author of two IoT books, 'IoT Disruptions' and 'The Internet of Things Business Primer'. Sudha teaches the first IoT Business course at Stanford Continuing Ed School. She hosts a weekly video show "The IoT Show". She shares a newsletter of IoT case studies that you can signup at http:// iotdisruptions.com

Sudha is a champion for Girls Who Code. She has been a venture mentor at MIT and Director of Bay Area Facebook, Twitter, Pinterest and Google+ Meetups. She also actively contributes to TechCrunch, Mashable, GigaOm and Venturebeat as a respected technology futurist. She is on the advisory board for Blockchain University and Barcelona Technology School.

Praise For Sudha Jamthe's IoT Books

"Sudha Jamthe's no-nonsense approach to IoT is refreshing, informative, and thorough. Read *The Internet of Things Business Primer* if you want to succeed in the IoT ecosystem." - **Ben Parr, Author of *Captivology* and one of Inc.'s Top 10 IoT Experts**

Sudha brings case studies from IoT Entrepreneurs and Product Builders globally and combines it with in-depth analysis from her own experience with Mobile Products to offer a must-read book about how to build a successful IoT Business. Watch out this is one of those books you are going to read and re-read many times to serve as your bible as the IoT ecosystem shapes out over the next few years."- **Myles Weissleder SF NewTech Meetup Founder**

"The Internet of Things Business Primer" is a guidebook for innovators, entrepreneurs and technology leaders looking for practical examples of best practices to build a successful IoT business. Sudha brings her own experience and the one of other entrepreneurs that have had a meaningful impact on charting the path of the IoT industry" - **Davide Vigano, CEO Sensoria**.

"Analysis of IoT from a business perspective by a seasoned business and product leader — that is what this book is all about. Sudha has done an amazing job in evaluating IoT and has shown us how to make a business out of it. This is not an easy task and

Sudha has done complete justice to it." - **Pragati Rai Sr Innovation specialist Deutsche Bank & Author Android Application Security Essentials**

"Sudha is an amazing thought leader in the new and exciting field of IoT. She is talented and inspiring with her words and work. Its exciting to see her put her deep knowledge of IoT and sharp vision of the future of this trend of technology into this book" - **Ahmed Banafa, Professor San Jose State University**

" We live in a connected world that continues to evolve each day. And therein lies the opportunity to build a business. Sudha Jamthe brings her years of experience as a technologist to this comprehensive guide, applying her own experience, and drawing from others in case studies that solidify important concepts. *The Internet of Things Business Primer* is a the definitive source for anyone looking to blaze a path in the IoT world and be successful doing it." - **Frank Gruber CEO and Cofounder of Tech.co and Author Startup Mixology**

"Sudha Jamthe's new book provides the definitive roadmap for building an IoT business and navigating the forthcoming disruption across many industries with a comprehensive overview covering technology, business models and use cases"

  — **Ajit Jaokar Author of Data Science for IoT and CEO Futuretext.**

"I really enjoyed Sudha's first book "IoT Disruptions" that covers the universe of opportunities that IoT is bringing to our lives. This book "The Internet of Things Business Primer" goes deeper to offer an in-depth guide and case studies for anyone who wants to learn how to build an IoT Business to accelerate the digital transformation."- **Josep Clotet, Founding Managing Director, Barcelona Technology School**

"Sudha is a great supporter of the grassroots of Silicon Valley. I had the honor to work with her, when developing Startup Weekend back in 2010 with eBay and PayPal. In this book Sudha is leveraging her unique insight to prepare the next wave of innovation and support the IoT community. This is not another book about IoT, this is a map on how to navigate the future of IoT entrepreneurship." - **Franck Nouyrigat. Co-founder Global Startup Weekend and Partner recorp**